Plans for small gardens

GEOFFREY K. COOMBS

(R.H.S. Garden Adviser)

LONDON

The Royal Horticultural Society

1979

Contents

Photographs: G. K. Coombs and Ernest Crowson
Plans: G. K. Coombs

Plans for Small Gardens

It is wishful thinking to suppose that in a book of garden plans a design can be found to fit exactly into one's own plot and fulfil all the requirements of a new garden, or perhaps meet the needs and revised ideas for one long established. It is, however, likely that certain sections and features can be usefully applied from a ready made plan or parts of several plans, such as arrangements for grouping shrubs and plants having regard for colour and spacing for specific purposes and places. The shape of a terrace for example could be taken in part from one plan and completed from another. Suggestions will be found for siting a greenhouse, garden shed and vegetables all of which are common ingredients of many gardens of differing size and shape.

The plans shown in this book are all commissioned works in response to definite conditions, and the photographs illustrate the finished results of theory put into practice.

Is a garden plan necessary? Not for some people with a wide knowledge of plants, a natural knack for visualizing the planting area and a great deal of time and energy to spend in the garden. But for those with less knowledge and much enthusiasm but with less time, that spent on drawing a plan is not wasted. It is easier to alter an outline on paper than on the ground and an overall view on a small scale is easier to assimilate.

On a site with no interesting features there are no decisions needed on what to save and what to remove, and we are free to plant what we want where we like. Where there are trees already well established it is not always easy to decide quickly which to keep, and I usually find that it is best to leave the decision until the design takes shape.

When a large garden has been split into several smaller units a large specimen may have to be related to a small area and although it is out of scale in the new environment one hesitates before cutting it down. In such conditions it is sometimes better to accept the large tree or shrub as the dominant feature, planting a lawn or bold groups of ground covering shrubs and plants that complement it in proportions and colour.

One aspect of garden design is the structural items such as walls, pools, paths and all features that are shaped and joined in the art of sculptured and quarried stone. The other is the plant material represented by trees, shrubs and plants and the variety of colour, shape and textures that are available.

With regard to colour schemes this depends to some extent on personal likes and dislikes, although there is still some choice.

For example if one wants to associate the pink rose 'Dearest' with a purple-leaved shrub there is a choice of a *Berberis*, a *Cotinus* or a *Prunus*

3

according to the shape wanted. Not only are the pink and purple colours put close together for specific effect but they may be combined with silver and blue in the same section of border. To eliminate any one would diminish the effectiveness of the planting scheme. In a garden where visual effect is the first consideration it is less important that the plant is uncommon than that it produces a good splash of colour. The gardener who collects plants because they are rare also requires a garden that is beautiful, but the plants are often of unusual interest, and he would probably not plant for instance *Lysimachia punctata* for the sake of introducing something yellow.

Something should be said about "shape" with reference to plant material. The outline of the borders and variations in heights produced by carefully placed specimen trees and shrubs at certain places will constitute the framework for a design, a detail of which is illustrated in Fig. 1 and pictured in Fig. 2 by the simple shaping of a border and a narrow column-like tree towards the apex of the widest part of the bed which gives emphasis to a focal point.

Fig. 1. (Left). Curved outline of a bed's elevations and shapes to produce a point of focal interest.

Fig. 2. (Right). Detail of the edge of the border.

Spacing is a vital technique. Shrubs and trees must be given enough space to grow, otherwise the plants will become overcrowded and shapeless. By advance planning, i.e. drawing the planting plan on paper to scale and allowing enough space for development, this situation can be avoided. When the plant first arrives it is difficult to appreciate that a shrub only 2 feet high (60cm) could increase to three times its size in three years. A nursery catalogue that gives the height, spread and flowering time together with other information about plants will give a good idea of allowances to be made. A method that can be used in preparing a planting plan after the shape of the bed is determined, is to mark the position of each shrub with a cross, in the case of a single specimen determine the exact place on the paper and draw a line in a rough circle around it. This outlines the space required when the shrub is established after ten or fifteen years or perhaps longer. For example if the total width of a *Philadelphus* is 10 feet (3m), the circle around the cross should have a radius of 5 feet (1.5m), If the shrub next to it in the bed will grow to 8 feet wide (2.5), the plants should be positioned 9 feet apart (2.7m). This is of course a long term solution, and by doing things this way there is much bare ground round the newly planted shrubs.

There are several ways of bridging this interim period between planting and growing. One is to plant the permanent shrub in position first and then plant several more of the same cultivar around it to give a full look to the bed quickly, but marking these for removal as the shrub in the centre requires more room. Shrubs are not cheap so this is an expensive way of obtaining a garden that looks established, and there is also the chance that the removal of the extra shrubs will be forgotten when the appropriate time for removal comes, resulting in a jungle.

The ideal way of making a garden look established from the beginning is in the use of ground cover plants. In the bare ground between the shrubs plant drifts and groups of carpeters that will make a complete ground cover without competing with the larger plants. The specimen shrubs may also be shown to better advantage by the plants underneath if carefully chosen for colour of flowers and foliage (an example of this is the scarlet flowered *Rhododendron* 'Britannia' and *Saxifraga umbrosa*, the foam-like pink flowers of the latter combining well with the stronger tone of the rhododendron and the glossy green rosette of leaves making a dense carpet on the ground). Other easily propagated carpeters and therefore expendable are *Polygonum affine* 'Darjeeling Red' and 'Donald Lowndes', *Stachys* 'Silver Carpet', *Geranium endressii* and several cultivars of *Campanula*. Some of the plants that have been used primarily to cover the ground will be suppressed by the shrubs as they spread outwards but they will have made a most useful contribution to the border and in the open places some will remain and continue to grow.

Some shrubs make a much more significant feature if several of the

5

same are planted close together in order to make one bold unit, for example *Ceratostigma willmottianum*, the small growing shrub roses and hardy fuchsias. Depending on the size of the border many others can be planted in groups of three or more, the distances between the plants in a triangle being 18 inches to 2 feet apart (45 × 60cm) so that they join together making one substantial unit 6 feet across (1.8m) in a shorter time than if only one is planted. This practice can be adopted throughout the planting scheme and in large beds shrubs such as *Cotoneaster salicifolius rugosus* could be two or three feet apart (60-90cm) but allowing eight to ten feet (2.5-3.1m) on the outer sides for development.

Most shrubs benefit from judicious pruning at some time, if only to nip back a wayward branch to maintain a good shape; for many others regular pruning is essential to obtain good results and has some bearing on spacing because, although in theory if a shrub is allowed to grow naturally it will attain a certain height and spread, the size can be reduced considerably by annual and careful pruning.*

A typical example is *Buddleja davidii* which will eventually attain ten to fifteen feet (3.1-4.5m) with a gaunt open structure of branches but by pruning hard in March a well shaped shrub within the space of six feet (1.8m) is maintained. Other shrubs that do not normally need hard pruning can also be contained within a smaller space than natural growth demands.

Family gardens

It could be said that the garden is a place of common interest but diverse requirements and sometimes the different needs are so many that it may seem impossible to include them all within a small space. There is, however, usually a common theme in the necessity to produce an attractive and colourful garden that is easily maintained, the latter being particularly necessary with a growing family which is inclined to make demands on free time at weekends.

The principal ingredients for a labour-saving garden are in many respects the same as those for any gardens, consisting of flowering and evergreen shrubs, roses of all types and carpeting plants. But different age groups see the garden in different ways and those interested in climbing frames and swings will have little regard for the quality of the turf.

A sand-pit is often demanded by the youngest members of the family. This should preferably be in a sunny spot, but also near enough to the house for mother to be able to see what is going on.

Sometimes a place has to be found for a wendy house and it, too, should be in a sunny pleasant part of the garden and made a feature that is complementary to the whole design. Looking ahead, its usefulness will eventually decline and it should be so arranged that after the removal of

*For more about pruning and details on how to deal with individual species see *Pruning Hardy Shrubs* (Wisley Series No. 12).

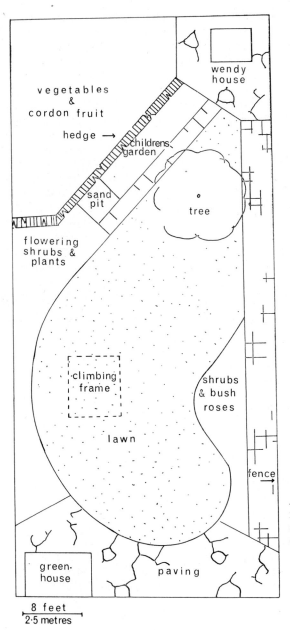

vegetables
&
cordon fruit

hedge →

childrens garden

sand pit

tree

wendy house

flowering
shrubs &
plants

climbing
frame

shrubs
& bush
roses

lawn

fence

green·
house

paving

8 feet
2·5 metres

Plan 1. A garden incorporating some of the needs of a young family.

the building the space can be planted and integrated with the rest of the garden. Another feature that should be situated near at hand is the children's garden where they can grow their own seeds and plants. The plot should occupy a favourable aspect and be likely to produce good results with little attention, otherwise the gardeners will be quickly discouraged. Small, easily maintained sections are best. In Plan 1 the children's garden is shown with a continous border 4 feet wide (1.25m) and bordered with a paved path. This could be divided into smaller areas by paving at right angles to the main path to make beds 4 feet square (1.25m²) which would be easier to maintain and different crops could be grown separately. It will be seen that the layout gives a good space for lawn and there is a dry hard surface from the house leading to the wendy house, sand-pit and vegetable garden. The borders of mixed shrubs and plants will give colour and interest at different times of the year, but bear in mind when making the choice that the young cricketer will sometimes score a boundary, and the goal-keeper will occasionally let a ball through right into the centre of a flower bed. At this stage in the garden's development it may be better to plant tougher shrubs and plants in preference to the rare and delicate. Roses can stand quite a lot of punishment from breaking, and even pruning down into the old wood sometimes produces new growth from parts that have been dormant for some years.

Concern is sometimes expressed, and not without reason, about poisonous seeds and berries and the injuries produced by some garden plants. One of the most dangerous in the latter respect is *Yucca gloriosa* whose sword shaped leaves end in a sharp spike. Not all yuccas are so vicious and they need not be eliminated from the list of invaluable foliage plants.

Some of the *Berberis* have many thorns that are brittle at the tips and break off immediately the skin is penetrated. But many give some of the best autumn colour and should not be banished from all parts of the garden; they can be used to very good effect to discourage persons taking short cuts.

Another dangerous plant is sumach (*Rhus typhina*), eventually making a small tree. The young branches are felted with tiny hairs which sometimes cause eczema if handled.

Regarding poisonous plants, laburnum seeds have received a good deal of publicity. This is probably the reason why laburnums are rarely planted as roadside trees although the upright outline of *Laburnum × watereri* 'Vossii' is particularly suitable. Similarly, the leaves and seeds of the yew tree will kill cattle in an hour or two, but there are many venerable yews both as hedges and specimen trees which have had a long and perfectly harmless life. The following list represents some of the plants commonly found in gardens that should be treated with caution. Berries and seeds to which children might be particularly attracted are marked thus*:-
Christmas rose (*Helleborus niger*); monkshood (*Aconitum napellus*);

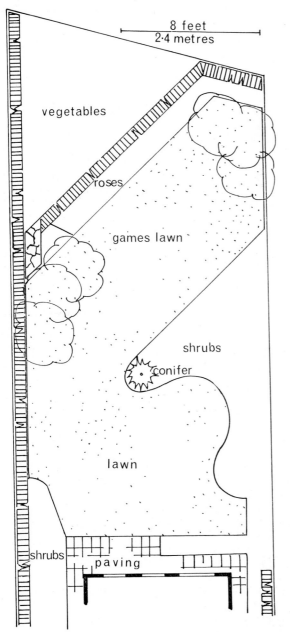

8 feet
2·4 metres

vegetables

roses

games lawn

shrubs

conifer

lawn

Plan 2. Making
maximum use of
grass space for
ball games.

shrubs

paving

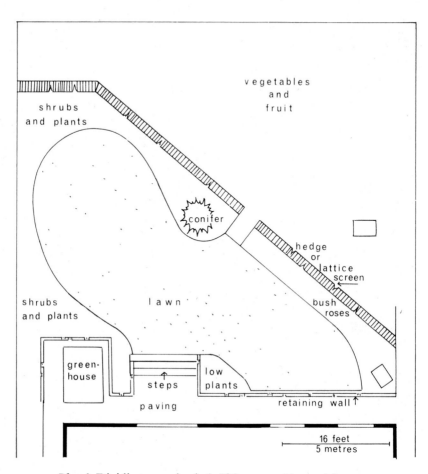

Plan 3. Dividing a garden in half for vegetables and flowers.

poppy (*Papaver*); daffodil (*Narcissus*); holly* (*Ilex*); spindle tree* (*Euonymus europaeus*); box (*Buxus*); laurel* (*Prunus laurocerasus*); ivy (*Hedera*); lily-of-the-valley* (*Convallaria*); columbine (*Aquilegia*); larkspur (*Delphinium*); lupins*; snakes head fritillary (*Fritillaria meleagris*); foxglove (*Digitalis*); mezereon* (*Daphne mezereum*); cotoneaster*; hawthorn* (*Crataegus*); mountain ash* (*Sorbus*).

The design in Plan 2 is basically very simple consisting mainly of one large border which at the widest part extends about half way across the garden. The primary object here is to provide plenty of room for ball games but at the same time to have an attractive garden. The long section of grass

10

is partly hidden by several bold groups of large shrubs and bush roses with low perennials in front on both sides to produce colour. The narrow conifer towards the apex gives an elevation at this point and the view between the conifer and the hedge on the left is emphasized towards the three ornamental trees near the entrance to the kitchen garden. The wide sweep of grass to the right disappears from view behind the border. This is always a feature worth aiming at in any design so that not all the garden is seen at a glance, but in this case it also provides the functional necessity of a large lawn. The long bed in front of the hedge which screens the vegetables could be planted with floribunda roses which would give a further touch of colour, the far end of which would not be seen from the house and terrace.

The diagonal line in a design may have disadvantages and be criticised for creating awkward corners particularly for an all square layout of a vegetable garden. In a rectangular garden, however, such a diagonal produces an illusion that the garden is larger than it is because it creates long views and in this garden has the longest possible area of grass.

Plan 3 also illustrates this method of dividing the garden into two equal parts, one for vegetables and fruit and the other for lawn and flowers. In this way there is an attractive view of the garden from all the lower windows of the house.

A plantsman's garden

The size of a garden has little to do with its quality and it is probably easier to maintain conditions of good cultivation in a very small garden than in a larger one.

The design in Plan 4 (p. 13) is the layout for a small garden* and includes several different conditions required for growing various types of plants. The ground slopes slightly up from the house and so a retaining wall has been planned on the left side of the garden immediately facing the house. The wall has been shaped so that a level area can be formed on which the garden shed and greenhouse can be built. The wall not only alters the lie of the land but the greenhouse and shed stand on a lower level than the lawn area and therefore the buildings are less conspicuous. The wall is at its highest near the house (probably not more than 18 inches) and diminishes to nil at the end near the entrance to the compost area. The cause of the wall diminishing is the upward slope of the paved path from the greenhouse, the top of the wall running level with the flower bed and lawn. The plants chosen for the beds will depend on the aspect. If one

*The same design was used for the Enthusiast's Garden, which is model Garden No. 3 at the RHS Garden ,Wisley. The planting is different, however.

wished to plant bush roses in the bed on the right side this would be suitable from a point of design; or they could be planted in the retained bed on the opposite side of the lawn if the aspect there was more suitable.

The rock garden is backed and flanked by shrubs and plants to give colour and foliage interest. Behind the rock garden the position might be suitable for *Cistus* × *purpureus* and *Juniperus virginiana* 'Grey Owl', or *Chamaecyparis pisifera* 'Boulevard' and *Genista lydia*. The crevices and spaces in this part of the garden are numerous enough to take many different plants and small shrubs that might be collected over the years. Evergreen shrubs to screen the compost area are *Mahonia* 'Charity' and *Ceanothus* 'Dignity', the latter is hardy enough to grow as a free standing shrub provided the locality is not too cold or exposed. Alternatives might be *Elaeagnus pungens* 'Maculata' and *Osmanthus* × *burkwoodii*. Lower shrubs worth a note are *Fabiana violacea, Euphorbia wulfenii, Coronilla emeroides, Daphne burkwoodii, Hebe* 'Pewter Dome', *Potentilla fruticosa* 'Elizabeth' and *Chaenomeles speciosa* 'Simonii'. Another place for rock garden plants is along the top and between the stones of the retaining walls and in a north-facing elevation which is not too dry the aspect is ideal for a collection of miniature hardy ferns.

The hedge on the left of the path should not be allowed to grow too wide and one possible plant is *Pyracantha* 'Watereri' which can be kept as low as three feet. Instead of a hedge, it can be trained flat against a wooden lattice. *Osmanthus* × *burkwoodii* is also excellent at a similar height. Beech is well known for hedge making, but it is seen less frequently mixed with an evergreen at the ratio of ten to one and looks particularly attractive in the winter. The hybrid holly *Ilex aquifolium* 'J. C. van Thol' is suitable for this mixture and is preferable to common holly because the leaves are less spiny and each plant fruits prolifically.

The broad border which takes the corner between the left of the steps and the greenhouse is intended to be planted with shrubs of not too great a density and only high enough to break the outline of the greenhouse and garden shed. Heavy shade is not usually required so near the house and the greenhouse should not be overshadowed. Shrubs to be considered are *Genista aetnensis, Ceratostigma willmottianum, Euonymus fortunei* 'Variegatus', *Rosmarinus officinalis, Lavandula* 'Vera', *Lavatera olbia* and *Spartium junceum*. The variety of shrubs and plants that could be grown in the different parts of the garden are too numerous to name. Instead of mixed shrubs, a heather garden or a collection of dwarf conifers could be planted in one of the beds, or in one of the narrower borders hemerocallis might be used instead of roses. Experimenting is part of the enjoyment of gardening.

The pool is associated with the rock garden, which has a cascade coming from between the rocks at a higher level and stepping stones to bridge the stream at the bottom.

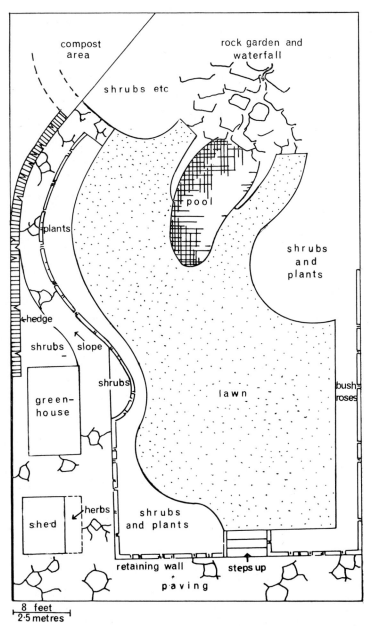

Plan 4. A connoisseur's garden for varied interests in the cultivation of plants, giving several different microclimates.

13

Water

A pool should be an integral part of the garden context, and the shape depends on whether it is incorporated in an informal layout or featured in an architectural design. The pool in Plan 4 is combined with the rock garden which has a water cascade coming from between the rocks at a higher level and stepping stones to bridge the stream at the bottom. The margins of the pool may be planted with waterside plants not demanding bog conditions such as *Iris sibirica*, *Hemerocallis* and *Rodgersia tabularis* because the ground around the pool would not be wet. In the water standing on a ledge, pickerel weed, *Pontederia cordata* and water iris, *Iris laevigatus* could be grown. This iris is considered by many to be the best of all the hardy water irises, and flowers principally during June and July. *Pontederia* forms large clumps which can easily be divided when they become too large; this plant produces attractive blue flowers. Other plants that are suitable for planting in water about a foot in depth are *Orontium aquaticum*, which has yellow and white spadices and flowers in May, and the Cape Pondweed, *Aponogeton distachyus*. This has floating leaves and produces fragrant white flowers throughout the year.

With regard to a fountain for those who prefer not to hear a continuous splash of water, the sound and ripples from a bubble fountain would be quieter and can be made by placing two large waterworn stones together, half submerged in the pool making a fissure from which water can be made to flow over and down the rocks; a way of introducing an interesting feature is to place two old millstones, if they can be found, one above the other, the lower one partly submerged in the pool with the water made to issue from the hole in the centre before splashing over the top and down the sides.

The possible danger of a pool to children may be decreased by placing a metal frame a few inches below the edge of the pool and above the water surface, to support chain link and wire netting over which can be spread several inches of shingle. The rock in the centre is embedded in the stones and the reservoir of water and pump to operate the fountain is concealed underneath.

Alternatively the advantages of a raised pool if it is retained about 18 inches (60cm), are that it is safer for children, and also makes a pleasant place to sit and watch the ceaseless life beneath the surface and the floating blossoms and leaves of water-lilies.

Plan 5 and Fig. 3 illustrate bold planting at the water's edge, with the sword-like leaves of the iris and the oval discs of water lilies providing interest.

* For further ideas see Wisley Handbook no 29 *Water Gardens* by Ken Aslet.

Fig. 3. Foliage texture and colour in a paved water-garden.

Informal paved gardens

The differences between a formal and an informal garden cannot always be sharply defined. In a formal garden the theme is a repetition of patterns, with beds of the same size and shape, and maybe with clipped hedges and topiary of box or other evergreen. Formal shapes can also be used in an informal manner, for instance in a paved garden, where there are different shapes and levels, and where balance is the important factor rather than equality. The garden shown in Plan 5 and Fig. 3 is about 50 by 60 feet (15.5 × 18m), and could just as well be ten feet (3m) more or less. Like any other garden it is not completely labour saving but it could be left for several weeks, even in the summer, without any obvious evidence of neglect. It will be seen from the plan list that everything is chosen to give colour and interest throughout the year with the minimum attention. The picture in Fig. 4 shows a part of a small garden that was entirely paved and it illustrates the informality of the planting which is a mixture of shrubs, roses, perennial plants and alpines that completely fill the borders and tumble out over the stone.

15

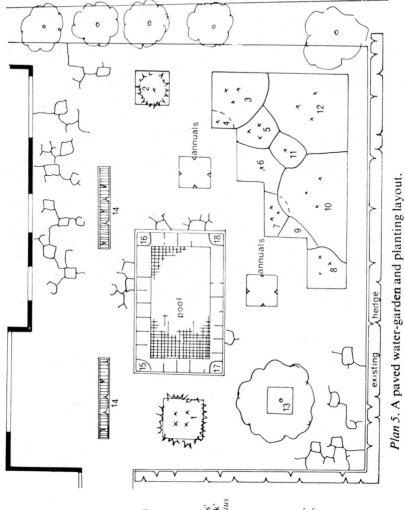

1. *Juniperus x media* 'Pfitzerana'
2. *Taxus baccata* 'Fastigiata'
3. *Cistus x purpureus*
4. *Yucca flaccida*
5. *Senecio laxifolius*
6. *Cistus x corbariensis*
7. *Salvia officinalis* 'Purpurascens'
8. *Genista hispanica*
9. *Helianthemum nummularium* 'Ben More'
10. *Escallonia* 'Edinensis'
11. *Deutzia* 'Codsall Pink'
12. *Cotoneaster salicifolius rugosus*
13. Standard *Crataegus monogyna* 'Pendula'
14. *Lavandula spica* 'Hidcote'
15. *Iris ochroleuca*
16. *Astilbe* 'Ceres'
17. *Iris sibirica*
18. *Astilbe* 'Red Sentinel' and *A.* 'White Queen'

Plan 5. A paved water-garden and planting layout.

16 feet
5 metres

16

Plan 6 represents a very small garden about 28 ft. square (8.5m²) and the beds are retained on three different levels, the small figure (No. 28) being at the highest point. The planting scheme shows No. 18 as a space for spring and summer flowers to be bedded out each year and this involves a small degree of maintenance, but the effort should be repaid by blossom from April to October. An alternative feature for the position could be a retained pool which would introduce movement and interest to the garden but less colour. If this was decided upon the accents of colour produced from flowers in the three urns would probably be sufficient and these elevations standing on the paving balance the retained bed and the whole design.

The raised lawn of chamomile produces a small sward of bright green against the colour of natural stone. Here too as an alternative the area could be finished level to the coping with a scree of pebbles, out of which low-growing and prostrate shrubs could be grown with their roots in the soil beneath.

See also Plan 7 (p. 19) for the use of paving in a narrow garden.

Fig. 4. Plants and shrubs breaking the edge of a paved garden.

17

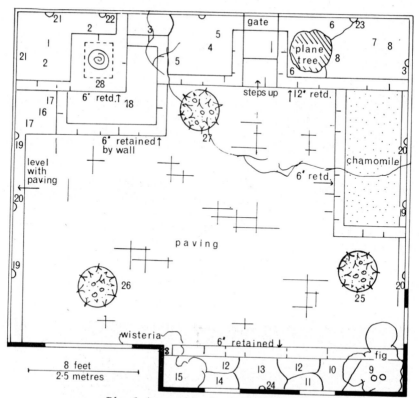

Plan 6. A paved garden and raised beds.

1. Camellia specimen, 4 feet, pale pink or white
2. *Euonymus fortunei radicans* 'Variegatus'
3. *Sarcococca confusa*
4. *Elaeagnus pungens* 'Maculata'
5. *Impatiens* F_1 Hybrids
6. *Vinca minor*
7. *Arundinaria murieliae*
8. *Vinca major* 'Elegantissima'
9. *Bergenia cordifolia*
10. *Senecio laxifolius*
11. Pelargonium (pink) for summer Wallflowers and/or bulbs for spring
12. Heliotrope for summer Myosotis for spring
13. *Fabiana violacea*
14. Pelargonium (pink) for summer Wallflowers and/or bulbs for spring
15. *Viburnum davidii*
16. *Hydrangea* 'Blue Wave'
17. *Polygonum affine* 'Donald Lowndes'

18. *Begonia semperflorens*, pink, 6 in. (15 cm)apart for summer. Tulips 18 in. (45 cm) high and Myosotis for spring
19. *Parthenocissus tricuspidata* 'Veitchii'
20. *Parthenocissus quinquefolia*
21. *Hedera helix* 'Goldheart'
22. *Hydrangea petiolaris*
23. *Hedera colchica* 'Dentata Variegata'
24. *Lonicera americana*
25. Flower urn on 2. ft plinth planted with spring and summer flowers
26. Flower urn, base resting on paving (no plinth) and planted as for preceding container
27. Flower urn on 18 inch plinth
28. Small figure about 3 feet high (90 cm) cast in reconstituted stone. The paving stones supporting the figure would be raised above the inspection cover by retaining walls.

18

1. *Cistus cyprius*
2. Climbing Rose 'Golden Showers'
3. Climbing Rose 'Swan Lake'
4. *Viburnum juddii*
5. *Euonymus fortunei* 'Silver Queen'
6. *Miscanthus sinensis* 'Zebrina'
7. *Philadelphus* 'Manteau d'Hermine'
8. Floribunda Rose 'Arthur Bell'
   Stachys 'Silver Carpet'
9. *Achillea* 'Moonshine'
10. *Campanula persicifolia* 'Snowdrift'
11. *Mahonia* 'Charity'
12. *Cornus albus* 'Spaethii'
13. *Hebe rakaiensis*
14. Floribunda Rose 'Iceberg'
15. *Anaphalis triplinervis*
16. *Pyracantha crenatoserrata* 'Knap Hill Lemon'—trained against fence
17. *Hypericum patulum* 'Hidcote'
18. *Cistus obtusifolius*
19. *Salvia officinalis* 'Icterina'
20. Climbing Rose 'Leverkusen'
21. *Phlomis chrysophylla*
22. *Stachys* 'Silver Carpet'
23. *Rubus calycinoides*
24. *Sambucus nigra* 'Aurea'
25. *Choisya ternata*—trained against fence
26. *Campanula porscharskyana* 'Alba'
27. *Buxus sempervirens* 'Elegantissima'
28. *Hemerocallis* 'Burning Daylight'
29. *Chaenomeles speciosa* 'Nivalis'—trained against fence
30. *Hemerocallis* 'Burning Daylight'
31. Climbing Rose 'Madame Alfred Carriere'
32. *Iberis sempervirens* 'Snowflake'
    Planting between items 28 to 32 could include:—
    Geranium sanguineum 'Album'
    Arabis albida 'Plena'
    Viola visseriana 'Lutea'
    Lysimachia nummularia 'Aurea'
33. *Jasminum officinale* 'Affine'
34. *Chamaecyparis pisifera* 'Filifera Aurea'

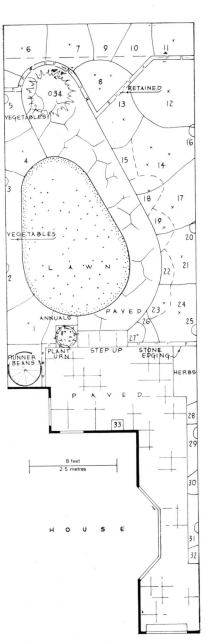

Plan 7. A garden where extensive use has been made of paving.

Narrow gardens

The charm of a garden may be its seclusion, and in a very small space this is not always easily achieved. In a large garden a grass walk may lead to a hidden arbour or a small lawn separated from the main part of the garden by a screen of shrubs. Plan 8 shows a very narrow plot 19 or 20 feet wide (5.5-6.5m) that has been divided into three sections. The one nearest the house with a lawn is the largest and the other two are hidden from view by hedges planted at right angles from the boundaries. Two important features about the design are the figure in the middle of the garden which gives a point of interest at the end of the path and seen from the house and terrace, and the sundial, in the same section, which is visible from the paving in front of the summerhouse. Both objects are borrowed to create focal points from two directions apart from an architectural function in the centre section.

The larger border that flanks the lawn could be planted with medium and small sized shrubs interplanted with two or three groups of floribunda roses. The narrow bed on the right side of the paved path might accommodate plants that like to sprawl such as *Gypsophila* 'Pink Star', *Nepeta* × *faassenii*, *Campanula poscharskyana*, *Alchemilla mollis* and a few more upright ones such as *Lavandula spica* 'Hidcote', *Agapanthus* and *Cheiranthus cheiri* 'Harpur Crewe'.

If, in the middle garden, the statue is raised upon a small plinth the surrounding bed could be planted with plants that would partially hide the base of the stone. A suggested colour scheme is white and blue flowers, no more than 2½ feet high (75cm) with grey leaved shrubs. The L-shaped border behind the sundial provides space for numerous plants. depending on the site conditions and aspect. In a cool lime-free soil a small collection of dwarf azaleas and rhododendrons interplanted with groups of lilies would be appropriate. Lilies are seen to advantage between low evergreens, the leaves of which seem to put the large blossoms into better proportion than with the meagre foliage provided by the lilies themselves.

If rhododendrons will not grow some of the hardy fuchsias probably will and the cultivars with large flowers which bloom from July onwards are 'Mrs Popple', 'Chillerton Beauty', 'Uncle Charlie' and 'Dr Foster'. Earlier in the season colour can be introduced by interplanting with campanulas and dwarf bulbs.

At least some of the shrubs and plants near the sitting-out space in front of the summerhouse should be fragrant and the following cannot be overlooked, *Viburnum juddii*, *Daphne burkwoodii*, *Lonicera* × *americana*, *Jasminum officinale* 'Affine'. A few plants bedded out annually, for the benefit of scent and worth the trouble are tobacco plants, heliotrope and ten-week stocks.

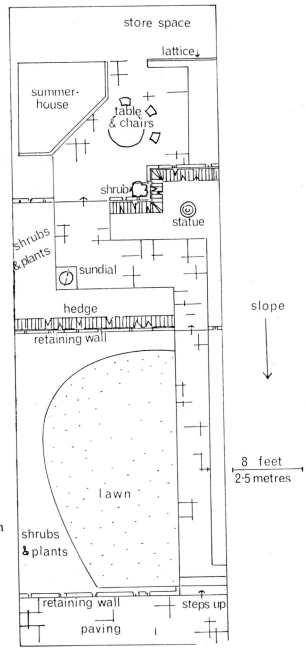

store space

lattice↓

summer-house

table & chairs

shrub

shrubs & plants

statue

sundial

slope

hedge

retaining wall

Plan 8. Three gardens in one narrow strip. This garden plan was the basis of Model Garden No. 1. at the RHS Garden, Wisley.

8 feet

2·5 metres

lawn

shrubs & plants

retaining wall

steps up

paving

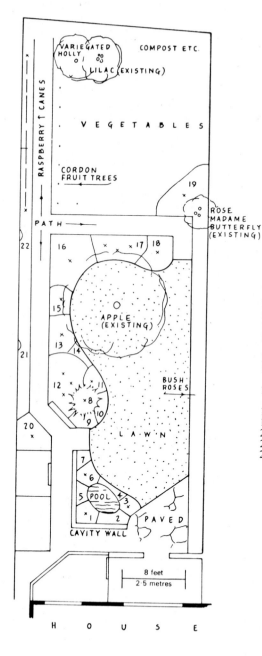

Plan 9. This narrow garden was planned to provide the following features: all the year colour and interest, a pool, and space for vegetables.

1. *Acer palmatum* 'Atropurpureum'
2. *Hosta fortunei*
3. *Hebe pinguifolia* 'Pagei'
4. *Saxifraga umbrosa*
5. *Hemerocallis* 'Burning Daylight'
6. *Juniperus sabina tamariscfolia*
7. *Bergenia* 'Evening Glow'
8. *Chamaecyparis lawsoniana* 'Ellwoodii'
9. *Stachys* 'Silver Carpet'
10. *Polygonum affine* 'Donald Lowndes'
11. *Senecio laxifolius*
12. Hybrid Musk Rose 'Wilhelm'
13. *Hypericum patulum* 'Hidcote'
14. *Polygonum affine* 'Donald Lowndes'
15. *Skimmia japonica* 'Foremanii'
16. *Elaeagnus pungens* 'Dicksonii' (existing)
17. Floribunda Rose 'The Queen Elizabeth'
18. *Mahonia* 'Charity'
19. *Cornus alba* 'Elegantissima'
20. *Daphne retusa*
21. *Cotoneaster lacteus*
22. *Pyracantha* 'Watereri'
Cordon Fruit Trees
Apple 'Sunset'
  ,, 'Egremont Russet'
  ,, 'Laxton's Fortune'
  ,, 'Lane's Prince Albert'
Pear 'William's Bon Chretien'
  ,, 'Conference'
  ,, 'Doyenne du Comice'
  ,, 'Glou Morceau'
Bush Fruit
Black Currants 'Seabrook's Black Improved'
Gooseberries 'Careless'
Raspberries 'Malling Promise'

22

The design of the garden in Plan 9 (opposite) is influenced by the apple tree situated in the centre of the garden. Features required in the layout are, all the year colour and interest, to walk round the garden without returning by the same route, a pool and space for vegetables.

Shade

Shade conditions can be divided into two main types; one occurs when the ground is in the shadow of a wall, which is often "moist shade" and the other is under trees where the soil is sometimes impoverished and dry.

The first mentioned does not pose a serious problem, and some plants actually require such a position. There are relatively few that tolerate the second category, but the following usually thrive successfully. *Hedera colchica* 'Dentata Variegata' is a useful ground cover and the lively variegated leaves bring life to darker corners. The ivy can be interplanted with groups of *Bergenia*, the large orbicular leaves and flowers of these combining well with the variegated foliage of the ivy. *Iris foetidissima* provides interest in the autumn with brightly coloured capsules of seeds and evergreen sword-like leaves through the winter. *Mahonia aquifolium, Symphoricarpus chenaultii* and *Lonicera pileata* contribute different foliage textures and the lemon yellow flowers of *Mahonia* are conspicuous in early spring.

Two thirds of the garden in plan 10 (p, 24) is overhung by trees and is in complete shade. The design and planting scheme should be appropriate for these rather difficult conditions, and a small lawn and paved area is incorporated in the sunniest part of the garden, Some of the plants used in this design are mentioned above, for example *Hedera colchica* 'Dentata variegata', which will form a dense ground cover under trees such as the *Crataegus* that was already well established in this garden. Other plants situated in the shaded area of this garden are the sweet bay, *Laurus nobilis* and the spotted laural, *Aucuba japonica* 'Crotonifolia'. *Hosta fortunei* and *H. sieboldiana* (nos 6 and 12 on the planting plan), will both thrive in 'moist shade', and their foliage provides a striking architectural feature during the spring and summer.

Plants in Plan 10 (p. 24).

1. *Juniperus sabina tamariscifolia*
2. *Hedera colchica* 'Dentata Variegata'
   Hedera helix 'Buttercup'
3. *Arundinaria murieliae*
4. *Bergenia cordifolia*
5. *Anemone hybrida* 'Honorine Jobert'
6. *Hosta fortunei*
7. *Cotoneaster lacteus*
8. *Laurus nobilis*
9. *Prunus padus* 'Plena'
10. *Aucuba japonica* 'Crotonifolia'
11. *Fatsia japonica*
12. *Hosta sieboldiana*
13. *Luzula sylvatica* 'Marginata'
14. *Elaeagnus pungens* 'Maculatus'
15. *Viburnum davidii*
16. *Hydrangea* 'Ami Pasquier'
17. *Sarcococca confusa*
18. Annuals
19. Annuals
20. *Mahonia* 'Charity'
21. *Hydrangea petiolaris*

* For further details see Wisley Handbook no 25 on 'Plants for Shade'.

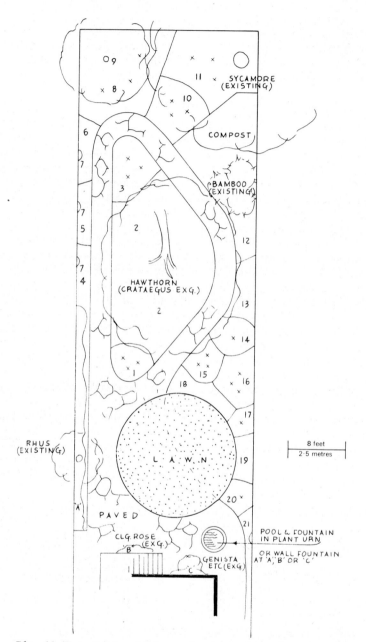

Plan 10. Two thirds of this garden is overhung by trees and in complete shade.

Fruit and vegetables

In a very small garden it is doubtful if space consuming vegetables, such as potatoes, are worth growing, and items that give a good return and occupy less room are to be preferred. Lettuce are easily grown and there is no comparison between one that is freshly cut and another that has had its growth terminated some time previously. It is also exciting to grow some of the less common items that are not usually seen in the shops.

Runner beans have the great advantage of thriving on the same site from one year to the next provided the ground is fed. When runner beans are supported by a pyramid of canes or similar means, the blossom and bold foliage of the vines can produce an attractive elevation in the flower garden. The foliage of beetroot is sometimes a useful foil for flowers, while another plant with spectacular colours and delicious to eat is Swiss Chard which can be grown in flower borders or in the vegetable garden.

Fruit trees in the form of 'cordons' (a cordon is a form of tree trained to a single stem) for apples and pears is a convenient way of growing them when space is at a premium and a good position is often adjacent to a path where they receive light and air, and pruning and spraying can be done easily at the appropriate times. Trained plum trees are usually grown in a fan shape and can be grown against a framework of wires and canes or against a wall or fence. If soft fruit is grown, necessitating a cage, it might be preferable to put all the fruit under protective netting. An example of the fruit section of a small garden may be seen in the model garden no 2 (Family Garden) at the Society's garden at Wisley. A diagram of the fruit and vegetable section of this garden is given on page 26; a key to numbered plants is given below.

Key (to diagram on p. 26).

Cordon Apples.

1. Sturmer Pippin
2. Ashmeads Kernel
3. Golden Delicious
4. Cox's Orange Pippin
5. Egremont Russet
6. Lord Lambourne
7. James Grieve
8. Red James Cave

Vegetables

1. (Seed bed)
2. Tomato 'Pixie'
3. Onion sets 'Stuttgarter Giant'
4. French bean 'Sprite'
5. Spinach beet 'Perpetual'
6. Salad onion 'White Lisbon'
7. Lettuce 'Unrivalled'
8. Beetroot 'Little Ball'
9. Lettuce 'Fortune'
10. Brussels Sprouts 'Peer Gynt'
11. Cabbage 'Hidena'
12. Carrot Nantes—Champion 'Scarlet Horn'
13. Parsnip 'Hollow Crown'
14. Courgette 'Green Bush F'
15. Cabbage 'Hispi'
16. Broad bean 'Kodrin'
17. Potato 'Foremost'

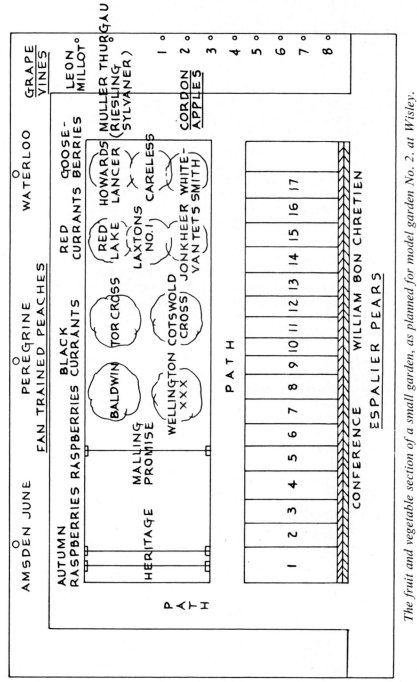

The fruit and vegetable section of a small garden, as planned for model garden No. 2. at Wisley.

Awkward shapes

To suggest that a design is typical of an awkward shaped plot would be a contradiction in terms because a garden of unusual shape and contour has characteristics and disadvantages and probably some advantages all its own.

Plan 11 is of a small front garden on a corner site where it is necessary to provide more parking space and extend the drive towards the front door. The position is made difficult because the ground slopes up fairly steeply towards the top corner of the garden but something more ambitious was required than retaining the bank by a single wall and planting with shrubs. In this garden it was not necessary to contrive split levels because they were dictated by the natural slope. It was decided to retain sections on different levels including an area of fine grass or chamomile. It might be said that it is inconvenient to lift a mower up 10 inches (25cm), but it should be no problem with the aid of a wooden ramp from the drive which can be placed in position and removed as required.

The garden in Plan 12 is an example of adapting the natural lie of the land to the design. This is a place where a rock garden is appropriate because the ground slopes up at about 45° at the end of the house, and bold outcrops of stone were placed in position. As a rule ,it is better to have a smaller number of large rocks than numerous small pieces. Most of the rocks should be well buried into the bank, say a third to a half in depth to give the effect of exposed strata forming terraces for planting alpines and dwarf shrubs. The bank on the left side of the drive is planted with shrubs. The lawn is the only flat part of the garden and is a suitable place for a bed of perennial plants, because the plants dictate some degree of formality and it does not seem right to see an herbaceous border on a bank. Even the herbaceous island bed is better on flat ground but its usefulness lies in the flexibility of its shape, and the shape can be made to co-ordinate with any adjacent outline. Greenhouses are sometimes difficult to place particularly in a garden that slopes upward where all vertical elevations appear to increase in height. If a greenhouse has to be in a conspicuous place, it is better to try to conceal it partially or it can be made an attractive feature, by buying a hexagonal one which is available in different sizes, constructed with wood or metal. In the general plan of the garden the view of the greenhouse is not unattractive seen from the lawn half hidden by shrubs above the rock-garden.

The garden in Plan 13 is less than a third of an acre but it is not small by standards of many gardens today. The aspect from the living room is relatively short and the shape of the design was dictated by the need for a fairly large vegetable garden. In addition the back of the house faces north. The longest views in the garden were those towards the top right corner, from thence back diagonally towards the house, and an equally long view

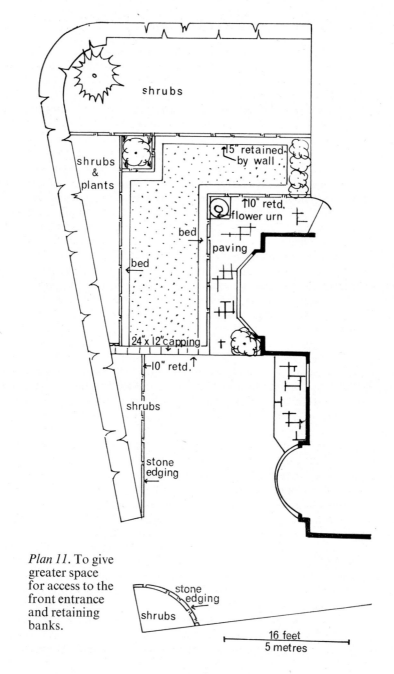

shrubs

shrubs
&
plants

15" retained
by wall

↑10" retd.
flower urn

bed

paving

bed

24" x 12" capping

←10" retd.↑

shrubs

stone
edging

Plan 11. To give
greater space
for access to the
front entrance
and retaining
banks.

shrubs

stone
edging

16 feet
5 metres

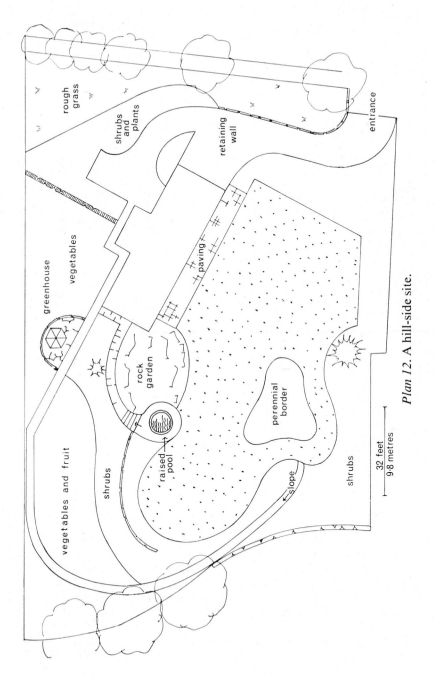

rough grass

shrubs and plants

retaining wall

entrance

greenhouse

vegetables

paving

rock garden

raised pool

perennial border

shrubs

slope

shrubs

vegetables and fruit

32 feet
9.8 metres

Plan 12. A hill-side site.

29

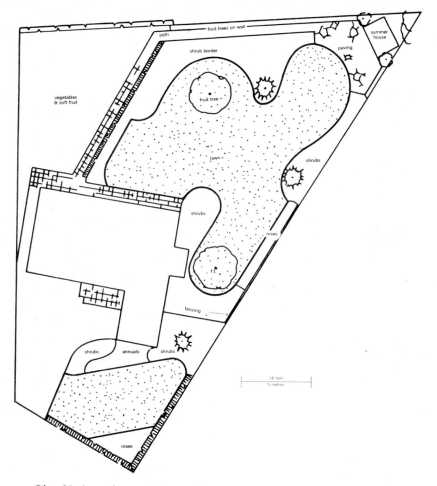

Plan 13. A garden requiring a fairly large section for vegetables and a summerhouse in a sunny position.

from the corner to the dividing fence at the side of the house and these different aspects have been used to advantage in the design. The vegetable garden is sited so that when the garden is established it will be hidden from view by a low hedge with the narrowest part of the plot behind the garage. Access is convenient from the kitchen for gathering vegetables and from the side of the house for transporting peat or fertilizer from the public road.

The summerhouse which happily occupies the sunniest part of the garden is seen from the house between two narrow conifers, one with glaucous blue foliage and the other golden. The rose border is seen equally well from the windows of the house and from the summerhouse. Another view from the summerhouse is a of broad grass section flanked with mixed borders and terminating with a specimen tree.

Both the standard trees in the lawn represent integral features in the design, they could be ornamentals such as *Robinia pseudoacacia* 'Frisia', *Malus* or *Prunus*, or fruit trees which are useful as well as decorative. The reason for putting them in the positions shown is because if an object is placed at a certain distance in front of a line, in this case the boundary, the space between the latter to the elevation will seem to increase because the eye first focuses on the nearest object. In both places the effect of greater depth is required.

The outline of the grass is in bold definite curves, sometimes terminating at a long straight edge giving definite shape to the lawn and augmenting the perspective of the garden.

Gazebos

A gazebo is not only for large gardens, although as it is usually placed on a hillock in a small garden it is as well to be sure that it does not overlook the neighbours. A gazebo can be an attractive feature, and could be substituted for the octagonal greenhouse in Plan 14 for instance, giving a view of the garden and the landscape beyond. There are many gardens with a similar situation.

Of the two plans shown (Nos. 15 and 16) the first is in a part of the

Planting plan for Garden No. 14.

1.	*Lavandula spica* 'Hidcote'	17.	*Iris foetidissima*
2.	*Daphne retusa*	18.	*Pulmonaria saccharata*
3.	Chrysanthemums	19.	*Geranium sanguineum lancastriense*
4.	*Cistus purpureus*	20.	Annuals—such as *Begonia*
5.	Kurume azalea 'Blaauws Pink'		*semperflorens* and *Impatiens*
6.	*Erica carnea* 'King George'		Hybrids
7.	*Anaphalis triplinervis*	21.	*Genista hispanica*
8.	*Sedum* 'Autumn Joy'	22.	*Bergenia* 'Evening Glow'
9.	*Hydrangea* 'Blue Wave'	23.	*Pentstemon* 'Evelyn'
10.	*Camellia*	24.	*Agapanthus* 'Headbourne Hybrids'
11.	*Hydrangea* 'Altona'	25.	*Hebe rakaiensis*
12.	*Camellia*	26.	*Fuchsia* 'Chillerton Beauty'
13.	*Juniperus sabina tamariscifolia*	27.	*Euphorbia wulfenii*
14.	Floribunda Rose 'Dearest'	28.	*Fuchsia* 'Mrs. Popple'
15.	*Viburnum davidii*	29.	*Senecio laxifolius*
16.	*Helleborus foetidus*	30.	*Eucalyptus*

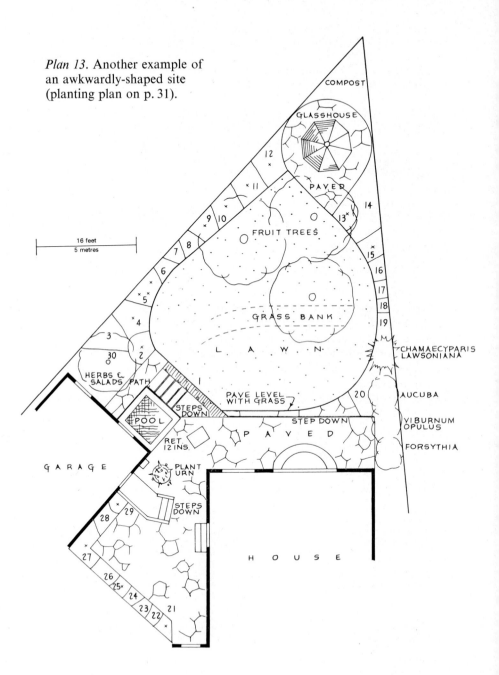

Plan 13. Another example of an awkwardly-shaped site (planting plan on p. 31).

COMPOST

GLASSHOUSE

PAVED

16 feet

5 metres

FRUIT TREES

CHAMAECYPARIS
LAWSONIANA

GRASS BANK

L   A   W   N

AUCUBA

HERBS &
SALADS PATH

VIBURNUM
OPULUS

PAVE LEVEL
WITH GRASS

FORSYTHIA

STEPS
DOWN

STEP DOWN

POOL

P   A   V   E   D

RET.
12 INS.

PLANT
URN

GARAGE

STEPS
DOWN

H   O   U   S   E

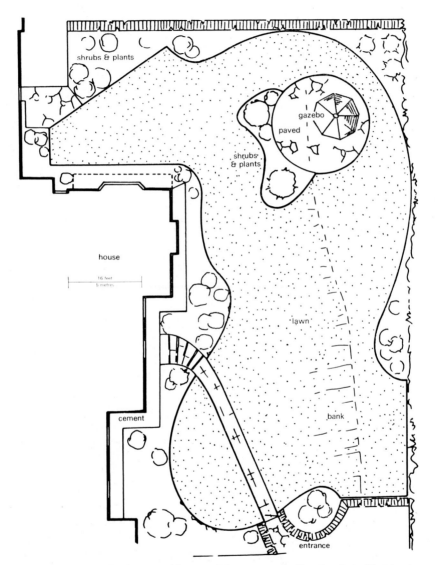

Plan 15. A gazebo is an architectural feature and a focal point of interest.

garden where the lawn slopes up to a rather featureless corner and the introduction of a structure gives a focal point of interest from the house and garden. The view from the gazebo, although not extensive, overlooks the flower borders in each direction. The circle on which the building stands is a plateau paved with stone, level with the grass at the back and three feet above the fall of the ground at the front.

In the other plan (No. 16) the garden extends in a long slope upwards and although the gazebo is built upon a circle of paving, the

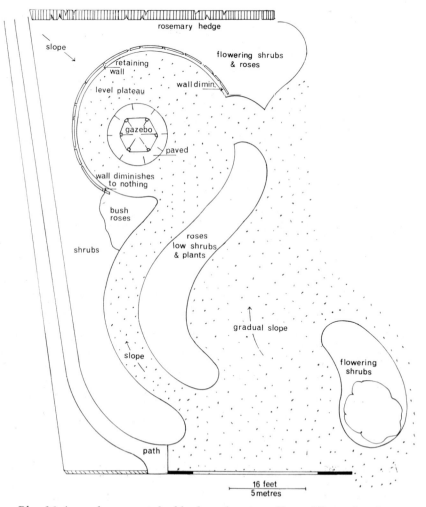

Plan 16. A gazebo approached by broad grass walks and flower borders.

grass and beds slope up to it at the front so no wall is visible at this point. The level space is produced by digging into the slope and retaining the soil with a wall at the back that diminishes to nothing at both ends.

Access to the gazebo is by a broad grass walk and it would seem that plants should be chosen to match the elegance of the building with Gallica and Alba roses and *R. centifolia* 'Fantin Latour', together with *Alchemilla*, lilies, *Hosta*, *Viola* and grey-leaved shrubs.

A rose garden

For the owner of a small garden roses are frequently grouped in separate beds or borders and contribute an abundance of blossom throughout the summer. Technically all roses are shrubs and many have found a permanent place in plant lists for mixed borders.

All the floribunda groups are extremely useful in a mixed border of evergreen and deciduous shrubs and some perennial plants. The rose 'Queen Elizabeth' for example will tower 6 feet or more (2m) at the back of a border, also its conterpart 'Scarlet Queen Elizabeth', 'Iceberg' (white) and 'Chinatown' (yellow). Nearer the front of the bed some shorter cultivars such as 'Dearest', 'Red Favourite' and 'Arthur Bell' produce a

Fig. 5. A rose border in a semi-formal setting.

35

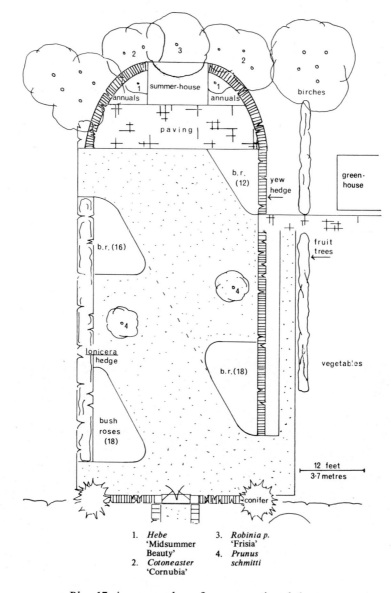

Plan labels within the figure:

- summer-house
- annuals
- annuals
- paving
- b.r. (12)
- yew hedge
- green-house
- b.r. (16)
- fruit trees
- lonicera hedge
- b.r.(18)
- vegetables
- bush roses (18)
- conifer
- birches

12 feet
3·7 metres

1. *Hebe* 'Midsummer Beauty'
2. *Cotoneaster* 'Cornubia'
3. *Robinia p.* 'Frisia'
4. *Prunus schmitti*

Plan 17. A rose garden of unconventional shape.

36

succession of pink, crimson and yellow flowers, in bloom from June to October. Hybrid Tea roses are different from floribundas in that they rarely look comfortable in the mixed population of a shrub border, except perhaps certain very strong growers such as 'Buccaneer', 'Peace', 'Eden Rose' and 'Uncle Walter', and in fact it can be said that these comparative giants, because of their size, are difficult to place in beds of shorter roses. Fig. 5 shows a border devoted entirely to roses consisting of several different cultivars and colours and although the layout is very simple there is just sufficient formality that Hybrid Teas seem to require without the geometrical patterns of repetitive shapes. In some rose gardens it is the practice to plant each bed with one colour and on a sufficiently large scale the effect is magnificent. When bush roses are part of the general layout, however, sometimes one of the most appropriate places for Hybrid Teas is adjacent to a paved area near the house, and in Fig. 5 where the bed is parallel in shape to adjacent lines of walls and paths it creates a semi-formal concept and does not look out of place as it might in another part of the garden. Roses in the foreground near the house should not be tall growers because not only will the rose bushes obscure the view but the heights are out of scale for beds say 4 ft. to 5 ft. wide (1.5m). Different colours are often grown in the same bed and the most satisfactory result is usually obtained by planting in groups of 3 or 5 of one colour and taking care to choose cultivars that are about equal in vigour.

Plan 17 is for a rose garden of rather unconventional design occupying an area about 80 by 30 ft. (23.5×9m) — the size of many small gardens although the plan shown is part of a larger garden with a secluded section for roses. A feature of the layout is that although it is effective as a rose garden it could also be taken as a design for a small ornamental garden and instead of planting only roses, shrubs and perennials could also be grown. Whichever planting scheme is adopted the shape of the beds produces an enlarging effect on the garden and the actual clear space through the centre is 11 ft. (3.3m) which will appear to elongate the distance to summerhouse from the gate. A similar effect looking from the other end, and the shaping of the beds, partially obscures sections of the grass in which two upright growing flowering cherry trees are planted. If all four beds are not devoted to roses two opposite sections could be planted with shrubs and perennials. Planted as a rose garden the beds are large enough to take enough bushes to give a good display of colour and one might be content to restrict the choice to four cultivars, or possibly as previously mentioned several groups of different colours in each bed. The areas of blossom seen from eye-level will appear closer together than on the plan, because the view of the beds is foreshortened, so there is far less visible break between one bed and another producing a greater mass of colour from the paving in front of the summerhouse and other parts of the garden.

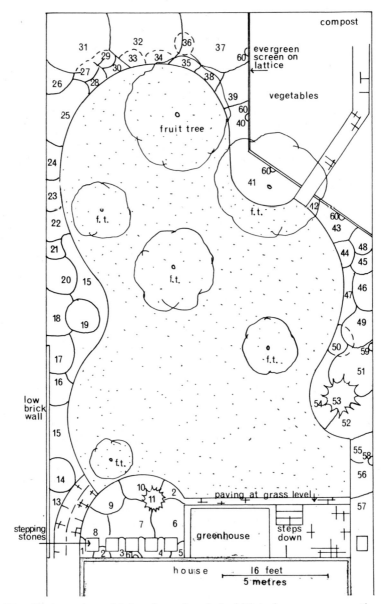

Plan 18. A garden with borders of varied width to increase perspective.

38

Key to plants.

1. *Viola gracilis* 'Lassie'
2. *Hebe pinguifolia* 'Pagei'
3. *Potentilla alba*
4. *Campanula portenschlagiana* 'Major'
5. *Erigeron* 'Elstead Pink'
6. *Fabiana violacea*
7. *Cistus purpureus*
8. *Rubus fockeanus*
9. *Genista lydia*
10. *Rosa chinensis* 'Nathalie Nypels'
11. *Chamaecyparis lawsoniana* 'Ellwoodii'
12. *Agapanthus* Headbourne Hybrids
13. *Cotoneaster dammeri*
14. *Viburnum davidii*
15. Lilies, Aquilegia, Epimedium, Hosta, *Potentilla alba*
16. *Euphorbia wulfenii*
17. *Euonymus fortunei* 'Variegatus'
18. *Coronilla emeroides*
19. *Mahonia* 'Charity'
20. *Viburnum davidii*
21. *Helleborus angustifolius*
22. *Pulmonaria saccharata*
23. *Heuchera* 'Scintillation'
24. *Saxifraga umbrosa*
25. Hybrid Musk Roses 'Penelope'
26. *Polygonum amplexicaule atrosanguinea*
27. *Campanula glomerata* 'Pixie'
28. *Helleborus niger grandiflorus*
29. *Anemone japonica* 'Margarete'
30. *Anemone japonica* 'Profusion'
31. *Cotoneaster salicifolia rugosa*
32. *Viburnum plicatum*
33. *Lamium maculatum* 'Aureum'
34. *Pentstemon hartwegii* 'Garnet'
35. *Campanula nitida alba*
36. *Dicentra spectabilis*
37. *Elaeagnus pungens* 'Maculata'
38. *Pentstemon* 'Myddleton Gem'
39. *Leycesteria formosa*
40. *Phlox* 'Fanal'
41. *Bergenia cordifolia*
   Bergenia 'Evening Glow'
   Polygonatum multiflorum
   Doronicum 'Harpur Crewe'
   Rudbeckia deamii
   Geranium dalmaticum
   Viola odorata 'Marie Louise'
   Viola odorata 'Czar'
42. *Polygonum affine* 'Donald Lowndes'
43. *Iris*
44. *Stachys lanata*
45. *Phlox* 'Sweetheart'
46. *Iris*
47. *Pentstemon* 'Myddleton Gem'
48. *Hebe* 'Midsummer Beauty'
49. *Spartium junceum*
50. *Senecio laxifolius*
51. *Cotinus coggygria* 'Royal Purple'
52. *Cornus alba* 'Elegantissima'
53. *Chamaecyparis lawsoniana* 'Green Pillar'
54. Floribunda Roses 'John Church'
55. Dutch Lavender
56. Hybrid Tea Roses 'Fragrant Cloud'
57. *Rosmarinus officinalis*
58. *Garrya elliptica*
59. *Ceanothus* 'Delight'
60. *Pyracantha* 'Watereri' trained against panels of lattice 4 feet high (1.2m)
61. *Ceanothus repens*

Small and square

In some ways it is easier to design a garden that is basically a square than a plot with boundaries that follow no particular line and are unrelated to the buildings. It is certainly much simpler to survey a plot without devious outlines and contours, on the other hand it can be said that something that is out of the ordinary demands an exercise in ideas and originality. But it is also a fact that in a small rectangular garden it is only the outside shape that is square and all the area that lies within it is clear for imaginative designing.

At first sight the boundaries are often too obvious but by thoughtful construction and shaping of the borders combined with a careful choice of shrubs and plants the sides can appear to be pushed out and the end of the garden to disappear. This has been achieved in Plan 18 (p. 38) which shows the plan of a small garden developed on part of an old orchard, the existing trees being only incidental. The design could be applied equally well to a vacant plot. The principle underlying the layout is to create a long diagonal view of the garden and this has to be achieved by the varied width of the borders and relating the fruit trees to the design. It also illustrates again that by not taking the vegetable plot right across the garden the view is not foreshortened and the boundary line encourages the eye to be carried towards the left side of the garden. The process is increased to even greater effect by the narrow conifer No. 53 because this is the first visual stop before seeing further into the garden. *Mahonia* 'Charity' (No. 19) on the opposite side also produces the effect of framing the more distant part of the garden. Although some of the fruit trees are old they still bear good crops and it was also worth keeping one or two for their interesting and twisted shapes and as supports for climbers such as *Clematis jouniana*, *Vitis amurensis* and *Rosa filipes* 'Kiftsgate'. The greenhouse is a small lean-to type and the nearby border of shrubs and plants provides a link between the glass structure and the house.

Plan 19 is an informal layout for a micro-garden only about 40 feet long (12m) and again the theory is to prevent a direct view from the house towards the end boundary. Behind the bird table *Rosmarinus officinalis* makes a thick medium sized evergreen in the middle distance, next to a group of scented red roses and a lavender bush, which all seem appropriate neighbours for the small area of paving which catches the mid-day sun, and breaks the up and down view of the garden. The lawn specimen offers a choice of small trees within a limited dimension. The *Sorbus* on the lawn is a selected form of mountain ash but an alternative choice would be *Prunus* ×*hillieri* 'Spire' or *Malus* 'Else Rathke'. Because space is so restricted the division between the ground set aside for growing salad crops and the flower garden is made with cordon fruit trees planted 3 feet (90cm) apart. The framework for support is made by inserting posts into the ground at

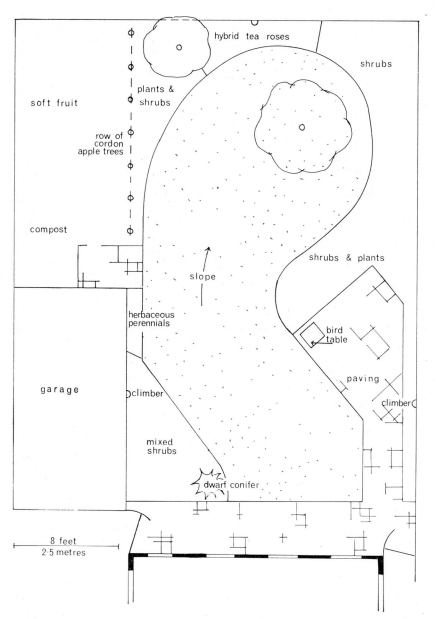

hybrid tea roses

shrubs

soft fruit

plants &
shrubs

row of
cordon
apple trees

compost

slope

shrubs & plants

herbaceous
perennials

bird
table

garage

climber

paving

climber

mixed
shrubs

dwarf conifer

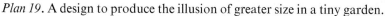

8 feet
2·5 metres

Plan 19. A design to produce the illusion of greater size in a tiny garden.

each end of the row to which are attached two wires, one 12 inches from the ground (30cm) and another about 4 feet above it; bamboo canes 7 feet long (2.1m) are then tied to the wires and the trees fastened to the canes. The plants immediately in front of the fruit trees are short and will not compete for light and nutrient.

The design in Plan 20 represents a small uncomplicated garden, very easily maintained but incorporating mixed borders of shrubs and peren-

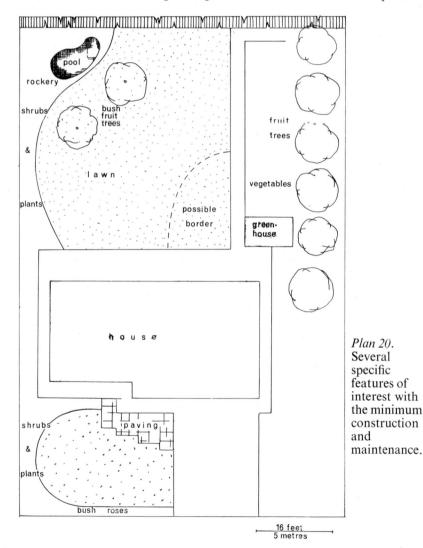

Plan 20. Several specific features of interest with the minimum construction and maintenance.

nials, a rock garden and pool, fruit trees, vegetables and a greenhouse.
The necessity for simplicity is partly dictated by a young family requiring
open space, the theme referred to in Family Gardens, but it is equally
applicable for someone who wishes to make an interesting labour-
saving garden. The suggested corner bed which is about 20 ft. by 12 ft.
(5.7 × 3.6m) reduces the grass area but produces the lawn in a more interesting shape, and the vegetables and greenhouse are partially hidden from
the house.

At the front of the house it is worth a note that the way to the front door

Plan 21. A plan to introduce emphasis to the front entrance and a simple
garden design.

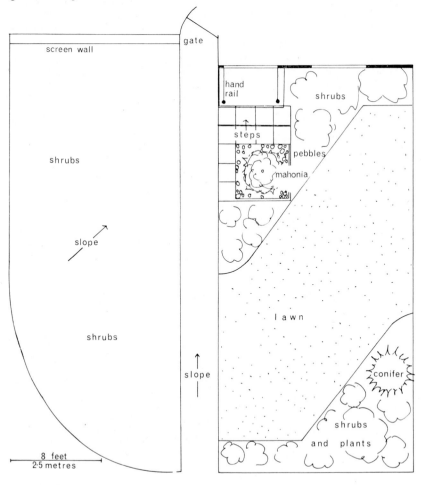

has been emphasized by paving across the corner between the entrance to the garage and the small path that leads at right angles from it. It is a common practice for building contractors to make the garage the most conspicuous feature on approaching the house, by making a wide and impressive expanse of concrete or asphalt that leads directly to it, with only a narrow path near the wall, apparently of no use for access to the main entrance.

Plan 21 also illustrates how the approach to a small house has been improved after imaginative thinking in the construction of the steps. The garden is a corner site and slopes up from the roads on two sides, the concrete path leads directly to the side of the house with only a high step at right angles from it to the front door. The plan shows how the un-inspired shape of the path and step have been used to make a position for an architectural feature and suggests a reason for the abrupt change in direction for access. The depth of the original step is reduced by making another step with a course of paving, thus reducing the height of the risers. A post and hand rail the same width as the top step on each side of the door gives a feeling of security on entering and leaving the house. On the same level as the path and corresponding to the slope paving of the same size is laid on two sides of a square which is edged on the other sides with concrete curbing the top of which is at the same level as the paving. Planted in the centre of the square bed thus formed is *Mahonia* 'Charity' and pebbles cover the area level with the surrounding stonework over which the leathery texture of the leaves stand conspicuously above the aggregate. The grass lines are purposely at variance to the square to give a relatively long section of grass and the design of the beds is made to take plants in some depth to produce a balanced layout with accents of colour and points of interest.

Naturalized gardens

There is no need to say that a so-called "naturalized" garden is not one where nature takes over, producing an abundance of flowers, growing at random from one season to the next and needing no physical effort, because a certain degree of attention is essential to prevent the short step back to the wild.

Two examples of a naturalized garden are the rock garden and heather garden. Both are types dealt with elsewhere and only mentioned here because in theory they typify a garden where the natural order of things is assimilated as near as possible under cultivation. Sometimes part of the garden consists of natural wood or coppice and it is here that a naturalized garden in the usual sense suggests places for shrubs and plants that require cosseting and need the protection of shade or partial shade. There are, however, several factors to consider such as the type of soil, whether it is alkaline, neutral or acid, retentive clay or porous sand, and the choice of

44

plants will naturally be influenced by these conditions. There are also rather less obvious problems in planting near trees; under a heavy canopy it can be dark and some plants will not tolerate drips from the branches, particularly beneath beech and many conifers. As well as poor light conditions, competition for water and nutrients can prevent newly planted shrubs and plants from growing if the ground is already full of fibrous roots from the established trees.

In adverse soil conditions it is possible to create pockets of fertile soil for the specific needs of particular plants by excavating an area of several feet across and 15 inches to 2 feet deep (30—45cm) or possibly more. The sides are then lined with thick polythene arranging it so that the top edge is level with the soil surface, and the hole filled with fertile soil.

Ivy sometimes covers woodland ground providing an attractive ever-green mosaic of leaves. Because of its invasive reputation it is sometimes regarded as undesirable and whilst the density of growth largely prevents weeds it also inhibits more welcome plants such as hardy cyclamen, ferns, snowdrops and other bulbs. Here too pockets excavated, lined with polythene and refilled with fresh soil will provide the necessary conditions. The practice of using the indigenous growth of the wood and concentrating on specific groups is sometimes better than clearing a site and exposing large sections of ground where cultivated plants will struggle to grow under the trees but weeds will flourish.

The surface of the paths that wander rather than having a direct course depend on whether the ground is hard or soft. If the soil is on the heavy side small shingle could be used without a definite edging of stone or brick with only low plants in groups to mark the edge so that the trodden path winds through plants instead of between shrub borders. If it is a sandy area probably no other material is needed and the track winds between dwarf shrubs and heather. The garden pictured in Fig. 6 was made in a partly cleared plantation of *Rhododendron ponticum* and birch trees and features broad grass walks that intersect different sections planted with groups of heather, azaleas, lilies and shrubs. The predo-minating plants in the island bed are the tall ornamental grass, *Miscanthus sacchariflorus*, yucca and bergenia making a bold group with emphasis more on shape than colour and equal in scale to the birch trees.

Plant associations

A miscellaneous collection of shrubs and plants unrelated in colour or form cannot be expected to produce the effect of those that have been grouped with a sense of awareness that different plants are more congenial as neighbours than others, even although some are diverse in shape and character. The border shown in Fig. 7 has produced a good show of flowers broken up by silver-grey leaved plants as a mediator between

Fig. 6. Broad grass walks in a semi-naturalized garden.

Fig. 7. An association of grey-leaved plants and flowers.

possibly conflicting colours. The short list given below is offered as examples of plant associations and a brief description of combined colours and foliage textures.

1. *Cotinus coggygria* 'Notcutt's Variety', *Cornus alba* 'Elegantissima', *Senecio laxifolius*, *Ceratostigma willmottianum* and Floribunda roses 'Dearest' or 'Arthur Bell'. *Colours:* deep purple foliage, grey-green and cream variegated leaves combined with grey-felted leaves, blue flowers, salmon pink or yellow roses; from early summer to late autumn. Red bark and grey leaves in the winter.

2. *Cortaderia selloana* 'Pumila', *Kniphofia uvaria*, *Salvia officinalis* 'Purpurascens'. *Colours:* grey-green arching leaves, silvery grey plumes with coral spikes, soft purple foliage, from summer to late autumn.

3. *Chamaecyparis lawsoniana* 'Columnaris', *Hebe rakaiensis*. *Colours:* glaucous blue foliage, apple green leaves; all the year round effect.

4. *Taxus baccata* 'Standishii', *Lavandula spica* 'Hidcote'. *Colours:* golden foliage, grey leaves and purple flowers; from mid-summer to autumn, evergreen foliage throughout the year.

5. *Kniphofia* 'Maid of Orleans', *Ceratostigma willmottianum*, *Anaphalis triplinervis*, *Hebe pinguifolia* 'Pagei'. *Colours:* cream, blue, white flowers, glaucous grey foliage; from early summer to late autumn.

6. *Fuchsia* 'Mrs. Popple' *Calluna vulgaris* 'Alba Plena', *Campanula portenschlagiana* 'Major'. *Colours:* carmine and purple, white, blue; from early summer to late autumn.

7̄. *Potentilla fruticosa* 'Elizabeth', *Nepeta×faassenii*. *Colours:* primrose yellow, pastel-grey foliage, lavender blue flowers; from early summer to late autumn.

8. *Bergenia* (all cultivars), hardy ferns, *Vinca major* 'Elegantissima'. *Colours:* mainly foliage, large bottle green or reddish bronze leaves, laciniate fronds, soft green edged with pale yellow variegated leaves, blue; from spring to late autumn.

9. *Cotinus coggygria* 'Notcutt's Variety', *Hippophaë rhamnoides*. *Colours:* deep purple foliage, silver leaves, silver twigs, orange berries; from early summer to late autumn.

10. *Cotoneaster dammeri*, *Hebe albicans*, *H. rakaiensis*, *Ruta graveolens* 'Jackman's Blue'. *Colours:* deep green foliage, flowers white, berries red, glaucous leaves, apple green leaves, opalescent blue foliage.

11. *Forsythia* or *Chaenomeles*, *Pulmonaria angustifolia*. *Colours:* yellow or pink and blue flowers; early spring.

12. *Buddleja davidii* cultivars, *Erica* and *Calluna*. *Colours:* purple, pink, mid-summer to late autumn.

13. *Rhododendron* 'Britannia', *Saxifraga umbrosa*. *Colours:* ruby-red, foamy pale pink inflorescence; late spring.

14. Floribunda rose 'Iceberg' or Hybrid Musk rose 'Prosperity', *Senecio cineraria* 'White Diamond'. *Colours:* white, silver-grey foliage with blue and mauve flowers; early summer to late autumn.

15. *Hamamelis mollis, Erica carnea, Colours:* yellow, purplish pink; mid-winter to early spring.

16. *Corylus avellana* 'Contorta', *Erica carnea, Colours:* yellow catkins, twisted branches, purplish pink; mid-winter to early spring.

17. *Cotinus coggygria* 'Notcutt's Variety', *Hedera colchica* 'Variegata'. *Colours:* deep purple foliage, blue-green, soft yellow variegated leaves.

18. Floribunda rose 'Iceberg', *Lavandula spica* 'Hidcote', Agapanthus Headbourne Hybrids, *Nepeta×faassenii. Colours:* white, grey leaves, purple flowers, blue and lavender blue flowers.

19. *Cornus mas*, muscari, *Erica carnea. Colours:* yellow, blue, purplish pink; mid-winter to early spring.

20. *Phygelius capensis* 'Coccineus', *Ceratostigma willmottianum, Senecio laxifolius. Colours:* scarlet, plumbago-blue, felted grey leaves.

The Royal Horticultural Society Garden Advisory Service

Members have the privilege of seeking the assistance of Mr. Coombs, the Society's Garden Adviser, who will give advice on all cultural problems. He will also assist with the preparation of plans for the alteration of the layout of existing gardens and prepare layouts for new gardens. A fee is charged, together with out-of-pocket expenses. Full details may be obtained from the Secretary, The Royal Horticultural Society, Vincent Square, London SW1P 2PE.

The Garden Adviser assisted by members of the Wisley Garden staff is in attendance at the Advisory Bureau, at all Shows in the Society's Halls.

Further ideas for small gardens will be gained by visiting the RHS garden at Wisley, where there are four small model gardens—Gardens for the Disabled, Enthusiast's Garden, Town Garden and Family Garden. In addition there are model fruit and vegetable gardens and model greenhouses for amateur gardeners.